HUNGER

A PLAY IN TWO ACTS

MEGHAN GREELEY

BREAKWATER
P.O. Box 2188, St. John's, NL, Canada, A1C 6E6
WWW.BREAKWATERBOOKS.COM

COPYRIGHT © 2022 Meghan Greeley
ISBN 978-1-55081-929-8

A CIP catalogue record for this book is available from Library and Archives Canada.

Cover image: Duncan Major
Dramatic series editor: Robert Chafe

We acknowledge the support of the Canada Council for the Arts. We acknowledge the financial support of the Government of Canada through the Department of Heritage and the Government of Newfoundland and Labrador through the Department of Tourism, Culture, Arts and Recreation for our publishing activities.

Canada Council   Conseil des arts
for the Arts   du Canada

Canada

Newfoundland
Labrador

Breakwater Books is committed to choosing papers and materials for our books that help to protect our environment.

For Ruth Lawrence,
a mover of mountains.

HUNGER

Hunger was first produced by White Rooster Theatre (in association with Rising Tide Theatre) at the LSPU Hall in St. John's, Newfoundland and Labrador, from November 18 to 21, 2015, with the following cast and creative team:

CAST

Johanna	*Ruth Lawrence*
Max	*Greg Malone*
Rivka	*Meghan Greeley*
Isaac	*Jamie Mac*
Helen	*Marthe Bernard*

Directed by *Michael Waller*
Produced by *Ruth Lawrence*
Set Design by *Lois Brown*
Lighting Design by *Jamie Skidmore*
Costume Design by *Melanie Ozon*
Sound Design by *Michael Waller*
Stage Management by *Mara Bredovskis*
Set Construction by *Karl Simmons*
Props by *Erin Normandeau*

It was remounted in 2019 by White Rooster Theatre and the Arts and Culture Centres of Newfoundland and Labrador for a provincial tour with the following cast and creative team:

CAST

Johanna	*Deidre Gillard-Rowlings*
Max	*Greg Malone*
Rivka	*Meghan Greeley*
Isaac	*Santiago Guzmán*
Helen	*Nina John*

Directed by *Michael Waller*
Produced by *Ruth Lawrence*
Set Design by *Lois Brown*
Lighting Design by *Jamie Skidmore*
Costume Design by *Melanie Ozon*
Sound Design by *Michael Waller*
Stage Management by *Emily Austin*
Set Construction by *Karl Simmons*
Props by *Erin Normandeau*

PLAYWRIGHT'S NOTE

While *Hunger* is set against the backdrop of war, it is about no war or conflict in particular; the play is strictly allegorical. Character names have been chosen to invoke allusions to literary or historical figures and are not meant to reflect or represent any one ethnicity, culture, religion, or geographical location. The grounds for persecution within the story are intentionally vague and open to audience interpretation, functioning best when they test our assumptions about power, class, education, gender, age, faith, ethnicity, or political ideologies. Similarly, genders prescribed to characters are included to indicate the lived experience of those characters but should not be prohibitive in casting.

CHARACTERS

JOHANNA	*A farmer. Woman, 40s.*
MAX	*A farmer. Man, 40s.*
RIVKA	*A musician. Woman, 20s.*
ISAAC	*A scholar. Man, 20s. Wears glasses.*
HELEN	*A child of wealth. Girl, 16.*

SETTING

Wartime. A period of persecution against unspecified groups of individuals. The location is a modest farmhouse in the countryside.

The recent past or not-so-distant future. Or now.

The house consists of one room, which is used for all things: eating, sleeping, living. In one corner is a bed. In another part of the room, a table and four chairs. Behind one curtained-off section is an area where a toilet and sink are, presumably, situated.

Against one wall is a dresser which, when pushed aside, reveals a small alcove. In the floor there is a trap door that leads to a tiny crawl space. It is covered by a rug.

Beside the front door there is a large bin for potatoes. On one wall there is a mirror. Beside the bed is an alarm clock.

There are several windows, curtained.

Ideally, the set should not be a literal interpretation of space—rather, an abstract suggestion of real space.

ACT 1

SCENE I

Afternoon. Late fall.

*MAX and JOHANNA sit at the table, soup in front of them,
not yet eating. There is a dish of bread on the table.
RIVKA and ISAAC sit on the floor, soup in front of them,
not yet eating. JOHANNA picks up a salt shaker and
passes it to RIVKA.*

JOHANNA: Guests first.

RIVKA: Thank you.

*RIVKA shakes the salt once over her soup. She passes
the shaker to ISAAC, who also shakes the salt once. He
passes it to MAX, who shakes the salt once. He passes it
to JOHANNA, who shakes the salt once. She pauses.*

JOHANNA: Would anyone mind terribly if I shook it twice?

ISAAC: Not at all.

RIVKA: Cook's privilege.

MAX: Go ahead, love.

*JOHANNA gives the salt shaker one more careful shake
and sets it down. She smiles brightly at RIVKA and ISAAC.*

JOHANNA: After you.

They all begin to eat.

JOHANNA: Is it all right?

MAX: It's a good soup.

JOHANNA: Not too oniony?

MAX: I don't think so.

JOHANNA: Rivka? Is it too oniony?

RIVKA: No. Not at all.

ISAAC: No, it's a very well-thought-out soup. Very balanced.

JOHANNA: Well then, I'm pleased you like it. I'm really pleased about that.

MAX: Not too cold down there, are you?

RIVKA: No, thank you, Max. It's quite nice, isn't it, Isaac?

ISAAC: It's a perfect temperature.

They eat.

ISAAC: Not too warm up there, are you?

MAX: Of course. It's terrible sitting up here.

RIVKA: Mmm. Chairs are so uncomfortable.

ISAAC: There's something so uncivilized about a table, isn't there?

MAX: Oh yes. Tables are for barbarians.

JOHANNA: You'll have to excuse our bad manners, then.

They smile at their shared joke.

JOHANNA: *(with an air of formality)* Can we barbarians offer you some bread?

RIVKA: *(copying her tone)* Oh, why yes, thank you, how kind.

They pass the bread around.

JOHANNA: Which way did you walk to market, Max? Through the woods or by the water?

MAX: By the water.

JOHANNA: Was it frozen?

MAX: Not cold enough for a freeze yet. Hasn't even snowed.

JOHANNA: Oh, I see.

MAX: *(tentatively)* Did you go outside today, love?

JOHANNA: *(ignoring him, to the others)* We go skating on the pond in winter. We always have such a lovely time of it.

MAX: Johanna, love?

JOHANNA: Hmm?

MAX: Did you go outside today?

JOHANNA: Let me think, did I go outside? I really can't remember. Did I . . . go . . . outside . . . Rivka? Isaac? Do you remember?

ISAAC: We didn't notice . . .

JOHANNA: I don't think I—no, you know what? I don't think I did.

MAX: Not even—down to the fence? To pat the dog?

JOHANNA: And oh, the dog! We always take the dog when we go skating on the pond. He loves it. Bernard loves it, he really does.

MAX: Bernard misses you.

Silence.

JOHANNA: Couldn't he . . . couldn't he just come inside, for a bit?

MAX: Johanna.

JOHANNA: It's just that—I was watching him from the window and he looked cold.

MAX: He see you looking?

JOHANNA: No. He was sleeping. I think he misses summer.

MAX: Dogs don't understand seasons.

JOHANNA: He moved around like he was dreaming.

MAX: They don't dream.

JOHANNA: How do you know?

MAX: Any creature that eats its own shit isn't smart enough to dream.

JOHANNA: Max, we're eating.

MAX: Anyway, you could have gone out to pet the dog at least.

JOHANNA *is silent.*

MAX: It's far away, love.

JOHANNA: Of course it is.

MAX: And it's quiet today.

JOHANNA: Mm-hmm.

MAX: We're all safe here—

JOHANNA: Anyway, what was I talking about? Before Max interrupted my story?

ISAAC: Skating.

JOHANNA: Yes! Skating. Do you skate?

RIVKA: No.

ISAAC: We never have.

JOHANNA: You'd love it. Someday we'll take you. Max and I, we always bring big thermoses of tea. And the radio! And we skate to the music. Don't we, Max?

MAX: Back when we had a radio.

Pause.

MAX: Johanna was so upset that we had to give it up. She's a real lover of music, you know.

JOHANNA: It was a silly rule. We should have refused.

MAX: They're illegal, Johanna.

JOHANNA: *(lightly)* A lot of things around here are illegal.

Beat.

RIVKA: May I trouble you for a glass of water?

JOHANNA: Oh . . .

MAX: What is it?

JOHANNA: The tap is broken, I'm afraid. Broke this afternoon, while you were out. Nothing to worry about, probably just frozen.

MAX: No, love, I told you. It isn't cold enough for a freeze.

JOHANNA: How do you know?

MAX: Science.

JOHANNA: We'll have to call the plumber, then.

MAX: The plumber's gone away.

JOHANNA: Oh dear.

MAX: You know anything about plumbing, Isaac?

ISAAC: I'm afraid that plumbing isn't one of the skills I learned at the university.

MAX: Pity.

JOHANNA: How will we manage?

MAX: Not to worry, love. Not to worry. There's the pond. And soon it will snow.

RIVKA: But you haven't got . . . any water in the house? Not a jug leftover?

ISAAC: There's no point in pestering, Rivka. If they haven't got it, they haven't got it.

RIVKA: It's just that I'm quite thirsty from the salt.

ISAAC: You'll survive.

JOHANNA: I'm terribly sorry. This isn't good hospitality, is it?

ISAAC: Not to worry, she's fine. Aren't you, Rivka?

RIVKA: Yes, I'm fine.

JOHANNA: Shall I clear your dishes?

ISAAC: Yes, thank you.

JOHANNA *removes the soup bowls.*

MAX: What does everyone say to dessert?

JOHANNA: Dessert?

RIVKA: Really?

MAX: When I was at the market, I bought dessert, special! Guess what it is! Something sweet!

JOHANNA: Oh, Max, I don't like to guess! What is it?

MAX: It's a surprise! Let's get out the good china, Johanna, what do you say?

JOHANNA: Of course! We have guests.

JOHANNA *gets the good china.* MAX *fetches something from a bag near the door.*

MAX: Johanna, you'll never guess who I saw today at the market!

JOHANNA: Who?

MAX: Guess!

JOHANNA: I don't want to guess.

MAX: I saw Katherine from on the hill. And you'll never guess what!

JOHANNA: What?

MAX: She's having a baby!

JOHANNA: Oh! Ooooh! Oh, that's so lovely.

RIVKA: This is a friend of yours?

JOHANNA: Oh, yes. She's a dear friend. We have so many friends, see. If we didn't, then perhaps you could sit at the table with us, but you never know who might pop by. You never know which of our friends might be coming this way and glancing through the windows.

MAX: And that's why we really shouldn't close the curtains. Not before dusk. It would look strange, you know?

JOHANNA: It's a little inconvenient, but what can you do when you just have so many friends?

MAX: Katherine says she misses you, Johanna. She says you should visit soon. When you're feeling better.

JOHANNA: A baby . . . I'm sure I'll visit her soon.

MAX: Maybe tomorrow?

JOHANNA: One of these days. When there isn't so much to do here at home. Besides, we have guests! It would be rude to leave them.

RIVKA: Oh, please don't stay on our account.

MAX: See? They don't mind. Do they?

ISAAC: No. Not at all.

JOHANNA: We shouldn't be rude, Max.

MAX: I can stay home one day.

JOHANNA: I don't mind staying.

MAX: Johanna—

JOHANNA: I don't mind.

The silence is awkward, but MAX *jumps to break it.*

MAX: Well, then! Ready for dessert?

RIVKA: Yes, please.

MAX *carries a dish towards the table, using his hand to veil what's on it.*

MAX: No last guesses?

RIVKA: I'll guess. Pastry?

ISAAC: Not these days.

MAX: No, it isn't pastry!

RIVKA: Cake?

MAX: No! It's . . . a . . .

MAX *moves his hand.*

JOHANNA: A sugar cube!

MAX: Surprise!

JOHANNA *lifts the sugar cube like a rare gemstone. They are all transfixed.*

RIVKA: I haven't seen one in . . . I don't know how long.

MAX: Hard to find, let me tell you.

JOHANNA: Were sugar cubes always so tiny? I remember them being bigger. Maybe that's a fantasy.

ISAAC: I think that's a normal size.

JOHANNA: I'll get a knife. We can all share it.

MAX: No need for that! No need for that! Everyone has their very own!

> MAX *sets the dish in front of* JOHANNA *and fetches the other dishes, each with a single sugar cube on it. He passes them around.*

MAX: Cherish them. I was told there won't be more.

JOHANNA: Was it expensive?

MAX: Well . . .

JOHANNA: How much?

MAX: Don't think about the price. Savour it.

> *They eat, except* JOHANNA.

JOHANNA: I think I'll save mine for later.

MAX: Yes, well . . . anticipation always makes a thing taste better in the end, doesn't it?

JOHANNA: I think I'll just like knowing that it's in the room.

ISAAC: Delicious.

RIVKA: This is very kind. We couldn't have asked for more gracious hosts.

> *She looks pointedly at* ISAAC.

RIVKA: Isaac, weren't you going to . . . ?

ISAAC: No.

RIVKA: But—

ISAAC: Rivka, that's enough.

MAX: Anything the matter, friends?

ISAAC: No. It's nothing.

RIVKA: It's just that—

ISAAC: Rivka.

RIVKA: May we have another candle this week?

ISAAC: We don't need another candle.

RIVKA: It's just—there's very little daylight that gets in, and there's so little to do to pass the time. Except reading, really. But once the candle goes out, we can't. It's much too dark.

ISAAC: No, it's fine. We're fine.

RIVKA: Isaac loves to read. He can read a book in a day, you should see it! He's always been a reader.

MAX: No trouble! No trouble! Still candles to be found at the market. You can just tack on the price to your rent and I will get a candle for you, no problem. Speaking of which—rent is due today, isn't it? I could get you one as early as tomorrow.

ISAAC: That's . . . the thing.

    ISAAC *retrieves an envelope from his pocket.*

MAX: I can take that off your hands, my boy.

ISAAC: I'm afraid . . . I'm afraid that we're a little short.

MAX: Pardon me? Sorry, my boy, I didn't quite catch that.

ISAAC: I said . . . I said that I'm afraid we're a little short. For this week.

MAX: Oh . . . oh, I see.

RIVKA: That can't be right, Isaac.

ISAAC: It is. We're in a bit of a predicament.

MAX: I see, I see . . . And am I right in thinking that, if you happen to be short this week . . . having no access to banks or alternative means of finance, that being short this week . . . means that you will be short each week hereafter?

ISAAC: I'm afraid so.

MAX: Meaning, I think, if I just take this a step further with some simple maths, that if you're actually short this week, having no access to banks or alternative means of finance, that next week, you actually cannot make the payment at all?

ISAAC: We're terribly sorry. If we had more, we would give it. But we're dry. We're completely dry.

MAX: Nothing . . . nothing for trade, even?

ISAAC: A few things, all of which are yours. My wristwatch.

RIVKA: (hesitates) I have a silver chain.

MAX: I see. I see.

ISAAC: We know those things probably aren't worth much these days.

MAX: Well, you can't put silver in the belly.

RIVKA: No.

JOHANNA: Oh dear.

MAX: This is, ah . . . This is terribly awkward, guests. I never do like talking about money. Especially not in these circumstances. It goes without saying, of course, that this . . . well, it violates the terms of our agreement, certainly.

ISAAC: We're so sorry. We didn't expect—we didn't expect to be here this long—

RIVKA: And there were so many weekly incidentals that we didn't anticipate—

MAX: Incidentals? Are you insinuating that we have in some way . . . taken advantage of you, friends?

ISAAC: No, of course not.

RIVKA: Absolutely not.

MAX: Your welfare is of the utmost importance to us.

ISAAC: We weren't insinuating anything.

MAX: No, of course not. Guests, would you mind returning to your quarters for a moment? So that I might have a private word with my wife? To discuss where we might go from here?

>   RIVKA *and* ISAAC *look at one another, nod.*
>   *Crawl towards the alcove.*

ISAAC: Thank you for the meal.

RIVKA *hangs back a moment.*

RIVKA: Please don't throw us out.

ISAAC: Rivka.

They crawl into the space. MAX *slides the dresser across. He and* JOHANNA *stand for a moment in silence.*

JOHANNA: They did seem to like the soup, didn't they?

MAX: Johanna.

JOHANNA: What?

MAX: This is very serious.

JOHANNA: Yes, of course.

MAX: And?

JOHANNA: And . . .

MAX: And?

JOHANNA: And good people are rewarded for their goodness.

MAX: Johanna, this isn't about being good—we aren't wealthy people. We'll starve. They'll starve. It's hard enough feeding us and the dog and the chickens. And the chickens haven't been doing well.

JOHANNA: It isn't about the money. It's never been about the money.

MAX: That's all well and good and lovely, but you know what doesn't put food in the belly?

JOHANNA: What?

MAX: Poverty.

JOHANNA: Don't be so callous.

MAX: My love, I'm not being callous. Of course I agree with you. Of course if there's selfless work to be done, it's work worth doing. But the world is a different place these days. And a selfless act is not currency. It can't feed us. It can't feed them. Those poor . . . my heart is breaking for them, Johanna. Haven't even got enough left for a candle.

JOHANNA: You're right.

MAX: I wish I wasn't, but I am. I am right.

JOHANNA: We can't turn them out.

MAX: No, of course we can't turn them out.

JOHANNA: They'll freeze before they starve.

MAX: Don't even speak of it. They're like family now. We aren't animals.

Pause.

MAX: I did hear a . . . well.

JOHANNA: What?

MAX: There was a . . . a whisper in my ear. So to speak.

JOHANNA: Who? Who whispered in your ear?

MAX: Might be better to not say.

JOHANNA: Oh. Yes, maybe better.

Pause.

MAX: Money, Johanna.

JOHANNA: How much?

MAX: Money worth the risk.

JOHANNA: Enough to feed us all?

MAX: Sounded that way.

JOHANNA: I feel selfish, thinking about whether I'll be fed.

MAX: Don't. A caretaker needs to be fed. A caretaker needs to be fed first, to ensure that all those in his care receive what they need and deserve. It's just practical thinking, my love.

JOHANNA: You're right. Of course, you're right. I can't help them if I starve to death, can I? Who will cook for them? They can't stand anywhere near the stove. It's too close to the window.

MAX: Exactly. And if I starve, there's no one to go to market, to replenish the stock. It'd trickle out after three days.

JOHANNA: You're right. You're absolutely right.

Silence.

JOHANNA: What now?

MAX: It has to be like we discussed.

JOHANNA: The second space?

MAX: Yes.

JOHANNA: Oh, Max. Is that the only way?

MAX: I think so. Can you think of another way?

JOHANNA: No.

Beat.

MAX: Well, now I'll just . . . it's just . . .

JOHANNA: What?

MAX: I hate talking about money. It's an awkward conversation. No way around it, I suppose.

MAX *slides the dresser across.*

MAX: Come out, guests, for a—a conference.

RIVKA *and* ISAAC *crawl from the alcove.* MAX *slides two chairs to that side of the room.* MAX *and* JOHANNA *sit in them,* RIVKA *and* ISAAC *at their feet.*

MAX: Have we been good to you, Rivka? Isaac? Have we taken good care of you?

ISAAC: Yes, of course. We understand the risk that you're taking.

RIVKA: And we're eternally grateful.

ISAAC: And we want to make it clear that even though we can't pay you now, when all of this is over, we will be in your debt. And we will find a way to pay you back.

MAX: Yes, that's—we appreciate that, certainly.

ISAAC: Name your price. We'll work, once this is over, tirelessly. To repay you for your generosity.

MAX: Ah, see, well. Here's the thing. That's a very beautiful promise, and Johanna and I, we'd like to accept it. But you have to understand that we—we're not—well, we come from a modest background.

ISAAC: Well, there's no shame in that.

MAX: No, no, well. My point is, we're not . . . we're not affluent people, you know? We haven't got stores of money and treasures lying around, to get us through.

ISAAC: I see . . .

JOHANNA: You have to understand that this isn't about our desire to do good.

MAX: No, we'd give you the shirts off our backs if that would help. But you can't eat shirts, can you?

ISAAC: No, of course not.

MAX: If we were rich, you know, we'd let you stay here for free. No question. But we aren't, and we can't afford enough to go around with nothing from you coming in.

RIVKA *buries her face in her hands.*

JOHANNA: Oh, no, don't cry! Don't cry! He hasn't finished yet. He hasn't got to the hopeful part.

MAX: I guess you could look at it as though that space you've been renting, that's a premium. That's a valuable little bit of real estate these days. And we just can't afford to let it go for free.

JOHANNA: But there is a solution.

MAX: Yes. And because that space is so valuable, we figure that we'd better not let it go to waste. Better offer it to someone who can afford that premium price.

JOHANNA: And just think! Another guest in the house. It's

like we're a growing family!

MAX: So, the way it stands, I suppose, you can consider this your notice.

RIVKA: But you aren't throwing us out?

ISAAC: Or turning us in?

RIVKA: We know there are valuable rewards. It must be very tempting.

MAX: Tempting!

JOHANNA: No, no.

MAX: We would never think of that.

JOHANNA: We told you, it isn't about the money.

MAX: No, don't insult us like that!

JOHANNA: We would never dream of turning you in.

MAX: Yes, imagine. Turn you over to that pack of dogs? Those barbarians? Not a chance!

RIVKA: Thank you.

MAX: Yes, see, we have a second space. One that we discussed using if things ever came down to it, you know?

ISAAC: Where is it?

MAX: Oh, don't think of that right now. We'll worry about that when the time comes. And so we'll take the wristwatch and the silver chain and get what we can for those and after that . . . well, we'll make it work, won't we?

ISAAC: Thank you.

RIVKA: Thank you so much. You have no idea.

> ISAAC *removes his wristwatch.* RIVKA *unfastens the chain around her neck. They each drop these into* MAX's *open palm.*

MAX: Is that real gold?

RIVKA: No, silver.

MAX: Not the chain. Your rings.

> RIVKA *and* ISAAC *look down at their wedding bands.*

RIVKA: No, please . . .

MAX: There's still a market for it, my dear. You can't eat vanity.

RIVKA: It isn't vanity. It's sentiment.

MAX: Can't eat sentiment either.

ISAAC: It's fine. We'll get new ones later.

> ISAAC *removes his ring.* RIVKA *removes hers, stops.*

RIVKA: Do you think . . . do you think we could hold onto them for another few days? Until we're really desperate? Then when the money from the wristwatch and the chain runs out, then you can take these and do what you need to.

> *Beat.*

MAX: Yes, why not? Now that I think of it, yes, let's do that. You hang onto them for safekeeping, and then when we really need the money, I'll take them. Go on, wear them for a few more days.

RIVKA: Thank you!

MAX: Yes, well. Better get back in now. You never know who's about on an afternoon like this.

RIVKA and ISAAC begin to crawl into the alcove.

MAX: Wait.

MAX goes to a spot in the kitchen. He produces a white candle. Offers it to ISAAC.

MAX: A candle for our special guests. Enjoy your book.

RIVKA: Thank you.

MAX: You're welcome. You're both welcome.

MAX slides the dresser across.

MAX: Well . . . I'd better head into town . . . make arrangements.

JOHANNA nods. MAX picks up his bag and exits.
Alone now, JOHANNA lifts the sugar cube. Brings it to her mouth. Changes her mind. Brings it to her mouth. Changes her mind. Lays it on the table. Looks at it. Looks at her finger. Puts her finger in her mouth and sucks on it.

Blackout.

SCENE 2

Several days later. Afternoon.

Classical music plays in the darkness. Lights rise.
JOHANNA *sits alone on the rug. In her arms is a transistor
radio, which she cradles like a baby.*

MAX: *(offstage)* Johanna!

JOHANNA *snaps the radio silent and pulls back the rug.
Beneath it is a trap door. She opens it, hides the radio,
replaces the rug. Makes herself busy.* MAX *pushes a
wheelbarrow through the door. The wheelbarrow's load
is covered in a cloth.*

JOHANNA: I didn't hear the dog bark.

MAX: Didn't. Sleeping.

JOHANNA *turns, sees the wheelbarrow.*

JOHANNA: Don't bring that inside! It's hard enough to keep
the floor clean.

MAX: Get the curtains.

JOHANNA: But it isn't dusk.

MAX: Quickly, Johanna.

JOHANNA *looks at the wheelbarrow, has a realization.*

JOHANNA: Today? Already?

MAX: Yes.

JOHANNA: I haven't prepared for it! I thought we had another week!

MAX: Change of plans.

JOHANNA: We haven't let them know.

MAX: Curtains, Johanna!

> JOHANNA *closes the curtains.* MAX *removes the cloth from the wheelbarrow, revealing* HELEN, *a young girl in a beautiful coat. She sits up, blinking.*

HELEN: Are we there?

MAX: You're here. Here you are! This—what did you say your name was?

HELEN: Helen.

MAX: Helen! Of course, Helen. This is my wife, Johanna.

HELEN: Pleased to meet you.

JOHANNA: Welcome, Helen. You're a brave little girl, aren't you?

MAX: Out you come, now, here you go. Back in a minute, can't have this sitting in the house. Looks strange.

> MAX *puts the cloth back over the wheelbarrow.*

MAX: Johanna, open the curtains, yes?

> MAX *exits.* JOHANNA *goes to the windows. She glances back at* HELEN.

JOHANNA: You had better sit.

HELEN: Where?

JOHANNA: On the floor. Out of sight, you know?

HELEN *glances at the floor.*

HELEN: It isn't very clean.

JOHANNA: Normally—normally it's very clean. That's from the wheelbarrow.

HELEN: May I sit at the table?

JOHANNA: Too high up, I'm afraid. If someone were to walk by the window, it would all be for naught.

HELEN *sits, gingerly, on the floor.*

JOHANNA: That's a very pretty coat, Helen.

HELEN: Thank you.

JOHANNA: What's it made of?

HELEN: I don't know. Wool, I think.

JOHANNA: Does it keep you warm?

HELEN: Yes. Though I didn't know I'd be travelling by wheelbarrow. I wouldn't have worn it, then. It's probably filthy.

JOHANNA: Small price to pay, isn't it?

HELEN: I guess.

MAX *returns, clapping his hands.*

MAX: It's a frosty one! Still not a flake of snow, though! Now, then!

A bomb explodes in the distance. MAX *and* HELEN *duck.*
JOHANNA hides under the table. The sound fades.
A moment of silence. MAX *stands and rubs his hands*
together as though nothing has happened.

MAX: Now, then!

HELEN *reaches into her bag and pulls out a china doll.*
She holds it close. JOHANNA *and* MAX *watch this.*

MAX: It's far away, Helen. Very far away.

JOHANNA *crawls from under the table, eyes on the doll.*

JOHANNA: What a pretty doll.

HELEN: Thank you.

JOHANNA: Does she have a name?

HELEN: Lucasta.

JOHANNA: Lucasta. I like that.

MAX: I would have thought you're too old for dolls, Helen.
Heart wants what it wants, I guess, eh?

HELEN: I've always had her. I couldn't leave her behind.
She's too special.

JOHANNA: Yes, of course.

MAX: Now, then! Are you ready to inspect your new
quarters?

HELEN: Yes. Thank you.

MAX: This house is haunted, you know.

MAX *winks.*

JOHANNA: Oh, don't tell her that.

HELEN: I don't believe in ghosts. I'm not twelve.

JOHANNA: He's teasing you anyway.

MAX: I'm not! We have two ghosts already. Two spirits living in the walls. Would you like to meet them?

HELEN: Is this a game? If so, I don't understand it.

MAX: No, no, not a game! No, I'm going to introduce you to your new neighbours, the ghosts!

> MAX *goes to the dresser and slides it across.* RIVKA *and* ISAAC *are sleeping.*

MAX: Wake up, sleepyheads! I can't believe the explosion didn't wake you already! You sleep like the dead, you two!

> RIVKA *and* ISAAC *rouse, blinking.*

MAX: It's moving day!

> *Silence.*

RIVKA: Oh.

ISAAC: Of course.

MAX: Helen, these are our tenants. Isaac, Rivka, this is our new guest.

RIVKA: Hello.

ISAAC: It's a pleasure to meet you, Helen.

HELEN: Hello.

MAX: Gather your things, my brave tenants.

ISAAC *and* RIVKA *each remove a small bag of items and crawl from the space.*

HELEN: Where are we all going?

MAX: You're not going anywhere, Helen. This is your new home.

HELEN *looks into the alcove.*

HELEN: In that dark little space?

MAX: When the dresser's pushed across, you'd never even guess it's there. Couldn't be safer.

HELEN: It looks a little dirty.

JOHANNA: Well, as you can see, the old tenants haven't had time to clean. It's short notice, you see.

HELEN: Does any light get in?

RIVKA: A little.

HELEN: What about air?

ISAAC: It's stuffy, but it's not bad. Though you can't let the candle burn too long. It eats the air.

HELEN: It's very tiny. I'm sorry, but I—I don't think Father knew how tiny it would be when he paid you.

MAX: Well, the tinier it is, the safer it is, really.

ISAAC: We managed with the two of us. It's not so bad.

JOHANNA: And you can spruce it up a little, if you want to. Make it feel like it's yours.

HELEN: I haven't brought anything for that.

MAX: Oh, come on, now, you'll get used to it! You'll get used to it. Better get in, now.

HELEN: *(hesitating)* May I stay out here for another moment?

MAX: We have rules about that, Helen. And it's already been too long today. You never know who might drop by unannounced, you know?

HELEN: *(indicating* RIVKA *and* ISAAC*)* They're still out here.

MAX: That's because we haven't showed them to their new place yet.

HELEN: Father's paying you an awful lot of money. He would like for me to feel comfortable and happy.

> *Pause.*

MAX: All right, you can sit over there by the wall for a moment. But stay close to the alcove. Understand?

HELEN: Yes.

> HELEN *goes to stand.*

JOHANNA: Helen, no!

> HELEN *freezes.*

MAX: I'm terribly sorry, but you can't stand. You never know who'll be walking this way and glancing through the windows.

> HELEN *sinks back to the floor. She crawls to the opening of the alcove. She turns and watches, holding her doll.*

MAX: (*to* RIVKA *and* ISAAC) Now, then, do you have all of your things?

ISAAC: Yes, everything. Are we going far?

RIVKA: Should we put on our scarves?

MAX: No, no, nothing like that. Not far at all! Never was a move more convenient.

> MAX *goes to the rug and pulls it back, revealing the trap door.*

JOHANNA: Wait, Max, I—

MAX: What?

JOHANNA: I . . . nothing.

> MAX *opens it.* RIVKA *and* ISAAC *crawl towards it and stare into the hole.*

ISAAC: You must be joking.

RIVKA: It's barely three feet deep. We won't fit.

MAX: I know you've been a little spoiled by the alcove, but . . . like we said, that space is a premium.

RIVKA: There must be somewhere else.

MAX: This isn't a mansion, is it? We're modest people who live within our means. We aren't blessed with hidden nooks and crannies.

ISAAC: No, we understand. We'll make do.

MAX: Friends, don't insult us like that. Please don't. We're working hard here to house you and feed you for practically nothing. It's hurtful, you know, when you complain, because we're doing the best we can. And that's not to mention the risk! You know what they do to people like us?

ISAAC: No, no, we understand, we'll make do.

MAX: All right, now, that's settled.

ISAAC: We will repay your kindness. When this is all over.

JOHANNA: We know.

MAX: Speaking of that . . . speaking of that . . . I'll be needing those rings now.

ISAAC: So soon? The money from the wristwatch and the silver . . . so soon?

MAX: Afraid so.

> ISAAC *removes his ring. He looks at* RIVKA, *who is still.*

ISAAC: It's just a ring, my love. It can be replaced.

> RIVKA *nods. Removes the ring. Lays it in* MAX's *palm. He holds them up.*

MAX: You know what these are? These are flour, potatoes, cheese in the belly.

ISAAC: Thank you.

MAX: All right, now. In you go.

> ISAAC *moves towards the crawl space. He looks at* RIVKA, *who is frozen.*

ISAAC: Rivka.

RIVKA: I can't. It's too small.

ISAAC: We have to.

RIVKA: I won't be able to breathe.

ISAAC: It's not forever.

RIVKA: We won't even be able to sit up down there. Our muscles will atrophy. And where will we—

ISAAC: What, love?

Pause.

RIVKA: It isn't very hygienic.

JOHANNA: It'll be the same as before. You'll still come out for mealtimes and . . . that. And have a little stretch. It'll be exactly the same as before.

ISAAC: Rivka.

RIVKA: I'm sorry, Isaac, but I can't. We're not animals.

ISAAC: Couldn't . . . don't you think that one of us . . . couldn't Rivka stay on in the alcove? It's large enough for two, we've proven that. It seems like a waste of space.

MAX: Well . . . I see what you're saying, I do, but it's a difficult thing to negotiate. That space is a premium, really, at a premium price.

JOHANNA: Oh, what difference does it make, when we have the money in hand? It makes no difference who sleeps where, does it? It should be Helen's decision.

All turn to HELEN.

MAX: . . . Helen?

Pause.

HELEN: My father paid for the whole alcove. It wouldn't seem . . . fair.

Silence.

HELEN: I'm sorry.

RIVKA: Please—

ISAAC: Rivka, can't you see she's frightened? Don't make her feel guilty.

MAX: Well . . . time is ticking. You best all be settling in now.

ISAAC: Rivka.

RIVKA *nods.*

ISAAC: I'll go first.

JOHANNA: Isaac.

ISAAC: Yes?

JOHANNA: . . . Never mind.

ISAAC *slides their bags into the tiny space. He stops.*

ISAAC: There's a radio down here.

MAX: A what?

ISAAC *pulls out the small radio. He hands it to* MAX.

MAX: Yes. Thank you. And tomorrow . . . tomorrow we'll discuss . . . well, since you're not paying us anymore, it might be helpful to Johanna if you could start doing some little things for her, to help her out. Nothing major, just some little things here and there. Simple chores and the like.

ISAAC: Yes, anything. We'd be happy to earn our keep. Thank you.

> HELEN *crawls into the alcove.* JOHANNA *slides the dresser across.* ISAAC *and* RIVKA *disappear into the crawl space.* MAX *closes the door.*
>
> *A moment of silence.*

MAX: *(indicating the radio)* What is this?

JOHANNA: Oh, yes. I'd forgotten about that one.

MAX: I told you to get rid of them both.

JOHANNA: That one doesn't work.

> MAX *snaps on the radio. Classical music plays. He snaps it off.*

JOHANNA: It's just a little radio.

MAX: It's illegal.

JOHANNA: A lot of things around here are illegal.

MAX: Do you know what the punishment is?

JOHANNA: I know full well what all the punishments are!

> *Silence.*

MAX: Put it in my bag.

JOHANNA: You can't sell it. You'll get caught.

MAX: I'm not going to sell it. I'm going to take it outside later and destroy it.

JOHANNA: Max, please don't.

MAX: It's not up for debate.

JOHANNA *takes the radio.*

JOHANNA: Can I just . . . could we listen to one last song, do you think? It couldn't hurt. Before you take it.

MAX: Johanna.

JOHANNA: Do you remember when we used to take the radio down to the pond? We'd listen to music and we'd skate for hours. We'd skate to the music.

Pause.

MAX: Fine. One last song, Johanna.

JOHANNA *snaps on the radio. Music plays.*

JOHANNA: When all of this is over, I'm going to buy a really good pair of skates, I think. Not the kind of blades that ꞁ you strap onto your boots, but the real kind. Those clean-looking white ones with the laces up the front.

MAX: Yes. And by then we'll have moved into town. And we'll skate on the artificial rinks, so we never have to worry about falling through thin ice.

The music plays. MAX *moves towards* JOHANNA. *He embraces her from behind. After a moment he tries to kiss her, but she subtly avoids it.*

MAX: All right, love. That's enough.

JOHANNA *switches off the radio. She opens* MAX's *bag.*
Something catches her eye.

JOHANNA: Max . . .

MAX: Yes, love?

JOHANNA: What is this?

MAX: What?

> JOHANNA *holds up a cloth from inside* MAX's *bag.*
> *She begins to unwrap the cloth.*

MAX: It's nothing, let me take that—

JOHANNA: What did you buy?

MAX: You really don't need to—

JOHANNA: Another surprise?

MAX: You mustn't protest—

JOHANNA: Why would I protest?

MAX: Or . . . well, you mustn't scream, you know?

JOHANNA: Why would I scream?

> *Pause.*

JOHANNA: Maximilian, why would I scream?

> JOHANNA *looks down at the cloth and unfolds it.*
> *It is a revolver. She withdraws her hand as though she*
> *has been burned.*

JOHANNA: What's it for?

MAX: Hunting.

JOHANNA: That's what hunting rifles are for.

MAX: I couldn't get a rifle.

JOHANNA: You shouldn't have sold yours.

MAX: You needed penicillin. And how was I to know there was a war coming?

JOHANNA: Everyone knew there was a war coming.

MAX: The doctor said you—

JOHANNA: I would have been fine.

MAX: It was an emergency.

JOHANNA: I would have been fine!

Silence.

JOHANNA: Anyway, you can't hunt. Everything's probably been scared into hiding by the noise.

MAX: All right, all right.

Pause.

MAX: It's for protection.

JOHANNA: Hide it.

MAX: It needs to be accessible. I might need it at a moment's notice.

JOHANNA: And why's that?

MAX: If anyone comes for a look-around.

JOHANNA: And what would that solve?

MAX: That'd be a figure-it-out-afterwards type of situation.

JOHANNA: Hide it.

MAX: How's a rifle different from a revolver?

JOHANNA: Hunting rifles aren't meant for people.

Beat.

MAX: I don't want to be questioned in my own home.

JOHANNA: "Hide it" wasn't a question.

MAX: I'm trying to protect us, here. Maybe you think this is all—all bigger batches of soup, but I understand a thing or two about reality, let me tell you. And I'm going to keep us safe.

Silence.

MAX: I'll hide it, love. By the door. In the potato bin, how's that?

JOHANNA: How did you buy this?

MAX: With . . . money.

JOHANNA: What money?

MAX: With the money from Helen's father.

JOHANNA: That was meant to feed us, Max!

MAX: There's no point in trying to feed us if—

The sound of a distant blast. MAX *drops instinctively to the floor.* JOHANNA *grabs the radio and dives under the table, gun still in her hand. They sit for a moment in silence. After a moment he gets up and speaks to her, still under the table.*

MAX: It's all right, love. Come out.

JOHANNA: What good is your gun for that, huh?

MAX: Pass it to me.

> JOHANNA *puts the gun on the floor, slides it out.*
> MAX *picks it up.*

MAX: And the radio.

> JOHANNA *doesn't move.*

MAX: Johanna.

JOHANNA: We're keeping the radio.

> JOHANNA *turns on the radio, the volume low. Music*
> *plays. After a moment* MAX *relents. He moves*
> *to the potato bin, places the gun inside.* JOHANNA
> *holds the radio like a baby.*

Blackout.

SCENE 3

Nighttime. Two months later. Complete darkness.

JOHANNA: Is it time?

MAX: I can't tell. Can't read the clock.

JOHANNA: Take it over by the window, might be a bit of moonlight. Anyway, it feels like it's almost time.

> MAX *moves in the darkness towards the window, an alarm clock in hand.*

MAX: We need to hold off to the last minute.

JOHANNA: I know, I know.

MAX: We can't run down the oil.

JOHANNA: Yes, I know.

MAX: There isn't more.

JOHANNA: Yes, I know that.

MAX: It's going to be harder now with the electric gone.

JOHANNA: You should have called the electrician.

MAX: Electrician went away.

> *Pause.*

> *There is a shift in the curtain. A sliver of dim light.*

JOHANNA: Is it?

MAX: My eyes are adjusting.

Pause.

MAX: It's time!

JOHANNA: Oh, good! Make sure the curtain's closed tight again.

JOHANNA *strikes a match and lights an oil lamp, which casts the room in a dim glow.* MAX *taps on the trap door, opens it.* JOHANNA *taps quietly on the wall beside the dresser, slides it open.*

JOHANNA: It's time! Everyone, it's time!

MAX: Wake up, guests! It's time!

RIVKA *and* ISAAC *emerge, groggily, from the floor.* HELEN *emerges from the wall.*

ISAAC: Time for what?

MAX: Time for what! Time for what! Listen to that, he's disoriented.

JOHANNA: It's almost midnight!

Silence.

RIVKA, ISAAC, *and* HELEN *stare at her blankly.*

MAX: . . . Of New Year's Eve!

RIVKA: Of what?

MAX: New. Year's. Eve. Poor things, they're groggy, aren't they?

JOHANNA *has brought four wine glasses to the floor.*
She is beaming.

JOHANNA: Aren't they beautiful? These are from when we were married. A gift from my parents. Long dead now, rest their souls.

HELEN *lifts one, inspects it.*

HELEN: Are they real crystal?

JOHANNA: Ah . . . no, 1 don't think so, no. Though I've never . . . 1 don't know.

HELEN: 1 don't think they are.

MAX: Too bad. We could have sold them, maybe, if they were. If it came down to it.

JOHANNA: They're pretty, though, aren't they? In spite of that?

HELEN: Yes, lovely.

JOHANNA *retrieves the water jug.*

JOHANNA: There's no champagne, unfortunately. Normally we do it right, don't we, Max? We usually have a bottle of champagne. And sometimes we go dancing.

MAX: No champagne for the last couple of years, though. Not with things the way they are.

JOHANNA: But there'll be champagne again when it's over. We'll get a bottle then, a good one. We'll get ten.

HELEN: What are we having instead of champagne?

JOHANNA: Rainwater. We'll pretend. Won't that be fun?

HELEN: Very.

JOHANNA: I wish we had a fifth glass. I'm so sorry. We don't mean to be rude. We'll have to share.

HELEN: That's okay, I don't want any water, thank you.

JOHANNA: Oh . . . but are you sure, Helen? It's New Year's Eve!

HELEN: I'm not thirsty, thank you.

JOHANNA: Very well . . . how much longer now?

HELEN: (*checking the clock*) Just a few minutes.

JOHANNA *pours the water into the glasses.*

RIVKA: (*to* JOHANNA) Rainwater—it hasn't snowed?

JOHANNA: Let me think, did I go out today? No, I guess I didn't. Max, has it snowed today?

MAX: Not a flake.

RIVKA: I've always liked the snow. I've never minded the winter. I like hats.

ISAAC: We got married in the winter. It was so cold that day that Rivka wore a white fur hat instead of a veil.

RIVKA: Our noses were bright red. It's a good thing that the photograph was black and white.

JOHANNA: Ooh, that's . . . May I see it? The photograph?

ISAAC: It was lost.

JOHANNA: That's a shame.

Silence.

MAX: Look at that! Almost time!

JOHANNA *distributes the glasses. They raise them in a toast.*

MAX: Here's to a new year.

JOHANNA: May this be the year that we see the last of it.

MAX: To a year of full bellies.

JOHANNA: To our brave guests.

RIVKA: To our selfless hosts.

ISAAC: To the perseverance of the human spirit.

HELEN: To our families far away.

MAX: To the coming peace.

JOHANNA: Tell us when to count!

MAX *regards the clock. He waits a moment and then makes a "come on now, hurry up!" gesture.*

MAX: Ten, nine, eight . . .

ALL: Seven, six, five, four, three, two, one . . . Happy New Year!

MAX & JOHANNA: Happy New Year!

They clink their glasses together. Drink. Hug each other.

ISAAC: This is excellent water.

They laugh.

RIVKA: Yes, honestly, this is the nicest water I've ever had.

JOHANNA: Goes down quite easily, doesn't it?

MAX: Yes, this water, you know, it's a very good year.

ISAAC: Someday it'll be a vintage!

They laugh as though tipsy.

HELEN: If I didn't know better, I'd think that water was going straight to your heads!

They laugh as though drunk.

ISAAC: Straight to my head? Straight to my liver, you mean.

RIVKA: Here, Helen, have some. Go on. You don't want to miss out!

HELEN: (*slyly*) You think Father would mind?

RIVKA: I think he'd understand that it's a special occasion.

HELEN *drinks. Giggles.*

HELEN: The room is spinning.

MAX: That was quick. First time?

HELEN: I feel as though I'm on a carousel.

RIVKA: That's called hunger.

ISAAC: I'm warm, for a change.

JOHANNA: Nice, isn't it?

MAX: Where's our manners, eh? Here we are talking about—about—about—weddings, and we haven't even asked Helen about—what about you, Helen? Do you have a boyfriend back home?

HELEN: Father said, he said, not till I'm seventeen.

MAX: What, and no boyfriend on the sly, eh? A sharp little thing like you?

HELEN: Well . . . maybe a couple.

ISAAC: A couple!

All cheer.

MAX: Ah, I thought so. A pretty thing like you, front of your dress filling out like that . . .

JOHANNA: Max! He's teasing you, Helen.

MAX: She knows I'm teasing.

JOHANNA: Don't mind him. He's a lightweight drinker.

They laugh drunkenly.

MAX: My wife's jealous.

JOHANNA: I'm not, I am not. Jealous.

MAX: Watch the way her cheeks flush when she gets jealous, eh? That's my bride, right there.

JOHANNA: They do feel red.

MAX: That's because, that's the blushing. Look how beautiful she is. I'm going to kiss her in front of everyone.

MAX *kisses* JOHANNA. *They cheer.*

ISAAC: Again!

MAX *kisses* JOHANNA *again.*

ISAAC: Should I do the same? I'm going to do the same, I think.

ISAAC *kisses* RIVKA. *They cheer.*

RIVKA: What about you, Helen, eh? You ever kissed a boy?

HELEN: Well, I'm not a baby!

RIVKA: Did you like it?

HELEN: Well, yes.

RIVKA: I remember those days. Soon you'll pick up where you left off, breaking every boy's heart. Come here, Helen, and give me a New Year's kiss on the cheek!

> HELEN *crawls to* RIVKA, *kisses her on each cheek.*

ISAAC: Well, don't I feel left out!

> HELEN *kisses* ISAAC *on both cheeks.*

MAX: And me!

> HELEN *kisses* MAX *on both cheeks.*

JOHANNA: And me!

HELEN: *(giggling)* The room's going around and around.

> HELEN *goes to* JOHANNA. HELEN *kisses her square on the mouth.*

MAX: That's a powerful water!

> *They all laugh as though intoxicated. Suddenly there is a whistle from outside, descending, like a sigh. The laughter fades. They sober up.*

ISAAC: What was that?

RIVKA: Was it the wind?

HELEN: Are there wild animals here?

MAX: Shh.

MAX *rises, goes to the window. He moves the curtain ever so slightly. Peers outside.*

JOHANNA: What is it?

MAX: Shh.

A tense silence.

JOHANNA: What is it, Max?

MAX: Shh!

Another tense silence.

MAX: Man with a lantern.

JOHANNA: Where?

MAX: Down the lane.

JOHANNA: Who?

MAX: Can't tell. Flashed it a couple times and put it out again.

JOHANNA: Bernard didn't bark.

The whistle happens again.

MAX: Lantern again. He's heading towards the house.

JOHANNA: I should put out the lamp.

MAX: Don't. That would seem strange.

MAX *hurriedly reaches for his coat, puts it on.*

JOHANNA: Where are you going?

MAX: He can't come here. I need to head him off.

JOHANNA: Be careful, Max.

MAX: Everyone, back. Now! Hurry!

HELEN crawls back into the alcove. JOHANNA *slides the dresser shut.* RIVKA *and* ISAAC *go towards the rug, pull it back.* MAX *heads for the door.*

JOHANNA: Take the gun.

MAX stops, reaches into the potato bin. He takes the gun, puts it in his jacket and exits.

JOHANNA: *(to* RIVKA *and* ISAAC*)* Hurry!

RIVKA pulls on the trap door.

RIVKA: It's jammed.

JOHANNA: No. No no no no no!

ISAAC: Let me try!

ISAAC pulls on the trap door, hard. It won't come loose.

RIVKA: Isaac!

ISAAC: It won't.

RIVKA: Pull harder!

ISAAC: I am pulling harder!

RIVKA: Both of us together, then!

They both try. It won't open.

RIVKA: Johanna, what do we do?

JOHANNA remains frozen.

ISAAC: Johanna!

JOHANNA *sinks to the floor in silence.*

RIVKA: The toilet.

ISAAC: There's just a curtain.

RIVKA: There's nowhere else.

ISAAC: The cupboard with Helen.

RIVKA: There isn't room for three!

ISAAC: What if there are dogs?

RIVKA: It's too late.

> ISAAC *and* RIVKA *race to the bathroom area.* ISAAC *freezes.*

ISAAC: The glasses.

RIVKA: What about them?

ISAAC: Four of them.

> ISAAC *and* RIVKA *race back. They each grab a wine glass. They disappear into the bathroom area, shutting the curtain behind them.* JOHANNA *is alone. She is still, breathing heavily. She gets up and moves to the window. She opens the curtain a sliver. Looks through. Closes it. Paces for a moment. Crawls underneath the table. A moment passes before* MAX *returns. He closes the door quietly behind him.*

MAX: Johanna.

> JOHANNA *is silent.* MAX *goes to sit on the floor beside the table.*

MAX: That was Henry from over the pond.

Silence.

MAX: Johanna.

JOHANNA: What?

MAX: That was Henry . . .

JOHANNA: What did he want on a New Year's Eve?

MAX: It's . . .

Beat.

JOHANNA: What?

MAX: Katherine on the hill.

JOHANNA: What about her? It's too early for the baby.

MAX: She and . . . they had a couple of them in the attic.

Silence.

JOHANNA: Katherine on the hill?

MAX: Katherine on the hill.

Silence.

JOHANNA: How did Henry know? They shouldn't have told anyone. He shouldn't have told you.

MAX: They were found out.

Silence.

JOHANNA: When?

MAX: Today.

Silence.

JOHANNA: Were they taken?

MAX: Shot.

JOHANNA: But what about Katherine? Surely a woman
with child . . .

MAX shakes his head.

JOHANNA: The baby.

MAX shakes his head. A glass shatters in the bathroom.

JOHANNA: The ones in the attic?

MAX: *(shakes his head)* Remarkable.

JOHANNA: How?

MAX: They got away.

Silence.

JOHANNA: That doesn't seem . . .

MAX: What?

JOHANNA: Fair.

*The curtain of the bathroom shifts slightly. RIVKA peers
out.*

RIVKA: Is it safe?

*No one answers. RIVKA and ISAAC emerge. RIVKA carries
something wrapped in a hand towel.*

MAX: Why aren't you down there?

RIVKA: The door was jammed.

ISAAC: I think the hinges need oiling.

JOHANNA: What was that noise?

RIVKA *unwraps the towel, revealing pieces of broken glass.*

RIVKA: One of the wedding glasses.

ISAAC: We're so sorry.

RIVKA: We'll replace it someday.

Silence.

JOHANNA: Bring me the radio.

ISAAC *goes to the potato bin, pulls out the radio.*

JOHANNA: Turn it on.

ISAAC *turns it on. "Auld Lang Syne" plays. He reaches under the table and places the radio in* JOHANNA's *lap. She cradles it like a baby.*

MAX: *(to* RIVKA *and* ISAAC*)* You should go back.

RIVKA: The hinges need oil.

MAX: There's only the lamp oil left.

RIVKA *and* ISAAC *look at the lamp, and then back to* MAX.

MAX: Turn it off.

RIVKA *and* ISAAC *look at one another.* RIVKA *goes to the lamp. Turns it off.*

Blackout.

The music plays.

ACT 2

SCENE I

Afternoon. Two months later.

JOHANNA sits with her feet up, drinking a cup of tea, her hair styled. She is dressed up (for her). RIVKA *and* ISAAC *scrub the floor.* HELEN *sits at* JOHANNA'S *feet, also drinking tea. The sound of a distant bomb. No one flinches.*

JOHANNA: You're safe here. Not to worry.

Pause.

JOHANNA: You know what I heard on the radio today? I can hardly . . . stacks of bodies. High as the house. And not enough earth to bury the dead. That could have been you, but no! You're here but for the mercy of . . . well, of Max and me, I guess. I guess—I guess because it's our mercy, in a way, isn't it? It's our risk.

Pause.

JOHANNA: As high as the house, can you imagine? All those brothers and sisters and mothers and lovers and friends. It makes me sick, right down to the bottom of my stomach.

Pause.

To ISAAC . . .

JOHANNA: Make sure you get what's between the boards, there. Dirt always sinks down between where the boards have split. It's always been such a nuisance.

Pause.

JOHANNA: Helen, do you like your tea?

HELEN: What kind of tea is it?

JOHANNA: It's regular tea, but with pond water. And stretched out a bit.

HELEN: With what?

JOHANNA: With, you know.

HELEN: No, what?

JOHANNA: With leaves and things. Do you like it?

HELEN: It's very earthy.

JOHANNA: Tell me about one of your events again.

HELEN: Which one?

JOHANNA: Your last birthday.

HELEN: Father threw me a large party.

JOHANNA: How large? How many guests?

HELEN: Thirty-two.

JOHANNA: And did you feed all of them? You had food for all thirty-two?

HELEN: Yes, of course.

JOHANNA: That's very generous. And what was on the menu, Helen?

HELEN: Duck with spring greens.

JOHANNA: Duck! That's nice. I had a duck one Christmas. A long time ago, now. And was there a cake?

HELEN: Yes, of course.

JOHANNA: What kind was it?

HELEN: It was a three-tiered plum cake with buttercream icing.

JOHANNA: Oh, my goodness. Aren't you a lucky girl! And I suppose everyone was dressed beautifully, for your party? All your little friends came in pretty dresses and all the boys in starched shirts and that?

HELEN: Mother gave me a new dress to wear. It was powder blue. And real silk. She said it made me look like a woman.

JOHANNA: I can almost picture it, Helen. Was there dancing? And music?

HELEN: Yes, of course. It was a party.

JOHANNA: I love music.

ISAAC: Rivka used to study music. Before.

   Beat.

JOHANNA: Oh, is that so?

ISAAC: Sorry. Didn't mean to interrupt.

JOHANNA: No, no, I want to hear about it. What kind of music, Rivka?

RIVKA: Classical. Strings. I studied the violin.

HELEN: It's looking a little dirty there, over by the dresser.

RIVKA: I'll get it.

JOHANNA: Do you have a favourite composer, Rivka?

RIVKA: It would be hard to say. I'm not sure that I could choose.

JOHANNA: I'm actually quite versed in music. Maybe you wouldn't think it, woman from the farmlands, but I am. I like Chopin, personally.

RIVKA: I love Cho—(*begins to pronounce it correctly, but adjusts to mimic* **JOHANNA**'s *pronunciation*) Chopin.

JOHANNA: I could have pegged you that way, had someone asked me.

> *Silence.*

> **HELEN** *takes a sip of tea.* **JOHANNA**, *watching her, also takes a sip of tea.*

ISAAC: You were listening to the radio today?

JOHANNA: For a half-hour.

ISAAC: Any news?

JOHANNA: I only listened to the news for a moment. Once I heard about the stacks of bodies, I changed the station. I prefer to listen to music on the radio. The news is always so grim. They never report about a happy thing, do they?

ISAAC: Probably not these days, no.

HELEN: Rivka, will you please be sure to scrub the floor of my alcove? I knocked a candle over yesterday and spilled a bit of wax.

Pause.

RIVKA: Yes, Helen.

RIVKA *moves to the alcove. She continues scrubbing.*

ISAAC: Pardon me—Johanna?

JOHANNA: Yes?

ISAAC: Will we eat, once we're done with the floor?

JOHANNA: Oh . . . well . . . there's nothing . . . Max has gone to the market. He'll bring something back for us all.

RIVKA: What about tea? May we have some of that when we finish?

JOHANNA: Oh . . . well . . . this is the last of the tea, I'm afraid. I scraped the bottom of the tin.

ISAAC: Are you sure there isn't any food here in the meantime? Anything small?

JOHANNA: Oh . . . well . . . let me just see, now.

JOHANNA *goes to the potato bin and opens it.*

JOHANNA: Well . . . no, look at that. No, I'm afraid there isn't anything.

RIVKA: When will Max be home? I'm feeling a little faint.

JOHANNA: Well, I can't read minds, can I? I don't know when he'll be back.

HELEN: Are you sure there is nothing at all? I'm starving.

JOHANNA *looks down into the bin.*

JOHANNA: Well . . . there is just the one . . .

HELEN: What is it? Is it a potato?

JOHANNA *reaches into the potato bin. She pulls out a minuscule potato, visibly rotten.*

RIVKA: I'll eat it. I don't mind.

ISAAC: No, me neither. We'll scrape around it.

JOHANNA: I suppose it's not that bad, is it? We can just . . . shave it a bit . . . and we could all have a bite. To tide us over.

HELEN: That doesn't seem fair.

All turn to HELEN.

HELEN: Well, it's hardly big enough to share. If everyone gets just one tiny bite, we might as well not have had anything at all.

JOHANNA: What do you suggest?

HELEN: Well, Father pays an awful lot of money for me to be happy and well-fed. And Rivka and Isaac . . . they don't really pay you anything. At all. So . . . if anyone should be entitled to the potato, it should be me, really.

Silence.

RIVKA: You little—

ISAAC: And what about Johanna? You're going to eat the whole thing and give her none? She's the reason you're still here.

HELEN: I think we should split it down the middle. Johanna and I.

JOHANNA: Yes, I . . . I suppose that's the fairest thing . . . it's unfortunate, Rivka, Isaac, but I don't . . . I don't see a way around it, really.

Silence.

JOHANNA *gets a knife. All watch as she sets the potato on the table and slices it in half. They look at the two halves.*

JOHANNA: How do we decide who gets which half?

HELEN, RIVKA, *and* ISAAC *crawl to the table to examine the halves.*

ISAAC: The one on the left is bigger. No question.

RIVKA: But it has more mould.

HELEN: We should flip a coin.

JOHANNA: We haven't got a coin.

ISAAC: Johanna should get first pick.

HELEN: Why?

ISAAC: Because it's her house.

HELEN: It was bought with my father's money. Besides, the person who does the cutting never gets to pick.

ISAAC: Says who?

HELEN: Says everyone. That's the rule.

ISAAC: I've never heard that rule.

HELEN: I can't help it that you weren't raised properly.

RIVKA: Shut up!

RIVKA snatches both halves of the potato.

HELEN: Hey!

RIVKA roughly pushes one half into HELEN's lap and the other into JOHANNA's hands.

RIVKA: There. It's been decided.

JOHANNA and HELEN eat their halves. RIVKA and ISAAC watch. HELEN sees this.

HELEN: Don't watch me! It makes me uncomfortable. You're supposed to be scrubbing my alcove.

RIVKA returns to the alcove, continues scrubbing. ISAAC picks up where he left off. JOHANNA and HELEN resume their tea-drinking positions. A brief silence.

JOHANNA: Did you ever go ice-skating, Helen?

HELEN: Yes, I was in lessons.

JOHANNA: You must be very good, then. I'm not—I'm not very . . . well, I've never been in lessons. But sometimes in winter I go skating on the pond.

HELEN: I hate ice-skating.

JOHANNA: Why?

HELEN: Because I hate cleaning the blades afterwards. Mother always used to make me do it, so that the blades wouldn't rust.

JOHANNA: I guess that part's a nuisance.

HELEN: It's a bore.

RIVKA *makes a strange choking noise.*

JOHANNA: Are you all right, Rivka?

RIVKA: Just dirt in my lungs.

JOHANNA: Try breathing through your nose.

HELEN: Can you do jumps?

JOHANNA: Little ones.

HELEN: Can you do a double axel?

JOHANNA: What's an axel?

HELEN: A turn-around jump.

JOHANNA: I can do a single axel, sort of. Why, can you do a double axel?

HELEN: I can do a triple axel. I got a medal once.

JOHANNA: Aren't you talented!

RIVKA: What's this?

JOHANNA: What?

RIVKA *turns with a letter in hand.* HELEN *sees this and makes a lunge for it.* RIVKA *evades her.*

HELEN: That's mine! I didn't give you permission to go through my things!

RIVKA: "Dear Father—"

HELEN: That's private! That's a letter to my father. You do not have my permission to read it!

JOHANNA: Oh, Helen, you poor thing. We could never get a letter to your father. It's too dangerous.

HELEN: Give it back!

ISAAC: Rivka . . .

RIVKA: "Dear Father. I miss you and Mother terribly."

JOHANNA: You poor thing.

HELEN: Stop it!

RIVKA: "You would be unhappy to know that I am living in a state of utmost squalor. The house is filthy and my hiding place is much worse. I am never allowed to sit at the table and instead the farmer and his wife force me to take my tea on the floor, like a dog. I shouldn't be surprised as their manners are quite subpar. They are terribly poor, and I fear the desperation of such poverty has driven them to cheat you out of an unreasonable sum of money in exchange for my supposed safety. Please hurry to find more suitable arrangements for me. Hugs and kisses. Helen."

Silence.

Stillness.

JOHANNA *then bends to collect the teacup and saucer that* HELEN *has abandoned on the floor.*

JOHANNA: I suppose you're finished with your tea, Helen?

HELEN: Johanna . . .

JOHANNA: The floor looks excellent, Rivka. Good work, Isaac.

HELEN: It wasn't what it—

JOHANNA: I think you've been out long enough today, don't you think? Better return to your respective quarters. For safety's sake.

RIVKA: Yes, Johanna.

> RIVKA *drops the letter in front of* HELEN. RIVKA *and* ISAAC *slide into their space beneath the floor.* JOHANNA *closes the trap door after them and replaces the rug. She turns to* HELEN.

JOHANNA: In you go.

HELEN: Johanna—

JOHANNA: I was thinking, Helen, about your age. How young you are. You're still a child, really.

HELEN: I'm sorry, Johanna.

JOHANNA: I was thinking that it might be a little inappropriate for you to call me by my first name. A little bit of formality might be more appropriate, given our age difference. From now on, I'd like you to call me Mrs. Darrow.

> *Pause.*

JOHANNA: In you go.

HELEN: Yes, Mrs. Darrow.

JOHANNA: Oh, and will you please pass me the candle from your alcove?

HELEN: Why?

JOHANNA: It concerns me to know that we've given you a candle and that you've wasted it on the floor. Not only are you being careless with something that's of great value these days, but you're also destroying my floor. This is not your home to abuse as you see fit.

HELEN: Please, Jo—please, Mrs. Darrow, let me keep the candle. It's so dark in there.

JOHANNA: Candle, Helen. Now.

> HELEN *places the candle in* JOHANNA's *hand.*

JOHANNA: Good afternoon, Helen.

> JOHANNA *slides the dresser down the wall. She removes the radio from the potato bin and sits at the table. She switches it on. Music plays.* JOHANNA *strikes a match, lights the candle. She watches it burn.*

MAX: *(offstage)* Johanna!

> JOHANNA *doesn't move.* MAX *enters. He stands by the door, an object wrapped in cloth in his arms.*

MAX: Johanna. The dog.

> JOHANNA *turns. Stares.*

JOHANNA: Frozen?

MAX: Starved.

JOHANNA: Put him on the table.

> MAX *sets the dog on the table. They sit for a moment in silence.*

JOHANNA: Did you go to market?

MAX: Yes.

JOHANNA: Did anyone buy our eggs?

MAX: There were no eggs today.

JOHANNA: Oh.

> *Pause.*

JOHANNA: Did you bring food home?

MAX: Slim pickings today, I'm afraid. Very slim. All very grim at the market. Couldn't . . . couldn't get a thing on the list. Not without a bit more money.

JOHANNA: There's nothing left here. I scraped the bottom of the barrel yesterday.

> *Silence.*

JOHANNA: Did the money come? From Helen's father?

MAX: Not until tomorrow.

JOHANNA: Oh, yes.

> *Silence.*

MAX: You shouldn't have the radio out.

> *Silence.*

MAX: Why do you have a candle burning? There's still a bit of daylight. It's a waste.

JOHANNA: It's not our candle. It's Helen's. I'm not wasting *our* precious things.

MAX: Why do you have it?

JOHANNA: I confiscated it for bad behaviour. I'm not sure that child's had the best mothering.

MAX: Still . . . we should conserve it, shouldn't we?

Silence.

MAX: Though . . . it's nice, in here. By candlelight.

JOHANNA: Yes. It makes everything softer.

MAX: That, and the music . . .

MAX *goes to sit on the bed.*

MAX: Why don't you come over here and sit beside me?

JOHANNA: I'm just going to sit here by the radio.

MAX: I can still hear it from over here. Or you could bring it.

Silence.

JOHANNA *doesn't move.* MAX *stands and goes to her. He kisses the top of her head. Tries to kiss her on the mouth.* JOHANNA *pulls away.*

JOHANNA: Don't.

MAX: Johanna.

JOHANNA: Not in front of Bernard.

MAX: How long will this go on for?

JOHANNA: I don't feel like it. The dog is dead.

MAX: And yesterday? And last week, when the dog was alive?

The sound of a bomb in the distance.

JOHANNA: Anyway, I couldn't. Not with that terrible noise. All the time now. Don't they ever rest?

MAX: We can turn up the radio.

JOHANNA: There's no music loud enough to make me forget about it.

MAX: You're not the first person who's ever lived through a time like this.

JOHANNA: No, and I'm sure I won't be the last.

MAX: *(hesitating)* Is it me?

JOHANNA: No.

MAX: What should I be doing?

JOHANNA: Nothing.

MAX: There must be something. I'm desperate, Johanna.

Silence.

JOHANNA: Desire's that strong, is it? All those animal urges coursing through your veins?

MAX: Don't make me out to be like that.

Silence.

JOHANNA: I was thinking that it's been quite some time since Rivka and Isaac had a payday.

MAX: So? We already have them doing chores.

Beat.

JOHANNA: I'm not the only one, you know.

MAX: What?

JOHANNA: I'm not the only woman in this house.

Silence.

MAX: Johanna.

JOHANNA: You haven't thought about it.

MAX: I . . .

JOHANNA: Hmm.

MAX: No.

JOHANNA: Rivka's very pretty.

MAX: I hadn't noticed, really.

JOHANNA: She's much more attractive than Helen.

MAX: Johanna—Helen's a child.

JOHANNA: She isn't, but she acts like one.

MAX: She's a child. That's not up for debate.

JOHANNA: But Rivka?

MAX: *(hesitating)* Isaac wouldn't hear of it.

JOHANNA: Probably not . . . Does it matter?

MAX: I don't know.

JOHANNA: Surely you must have noticed her. In these close quarters.

MAX: Johanna.

JOHANNA: Never considered it, not even for a moment?

MAX: Yes. What do you want me to say, Johanna? Yes. I notice her.

JOHANNA *nods as though satisfied.*

JOHANNA: Go on. It doesn't hurt to ask.

A kind of standoff. Then the trap door swings open. RIVKA *climbs out.* MAX *and* JOHANNA *stare at her.*

RIVKA: What, you think sound doesn't travel through your thin floors?

Silence.

MAX: Isaac?

RIVKA: Sleeping. All he does is sleep. All he can do is sleep, lying horizontally twenty-three hours a day. Our thighs are like jelly.

JOHANNA: What did you hear?

RIVKA: I heard everything.

Pause.

JOHANNA: And?

MAX: Johanna . . .

RIVKA: Good potatoes for a week.

JOHANNA: We can't promise that there will be potatoes. You know that.

MAX: Johanna.

JOHANNA: What?

MAX: I don't want to have this conversation.

JOHANNA: Then stand over there so you don't have to.

MAX: But—

JOHANNA: Do as I say, Max.

> MAX *relents. He shuffles awkwardly to one side.*

RIVKA: I want the alcove back. The brat can trade with us.

JOHANNA: Helen's father has paid for that alcove. I'm not in a position to barter with it.

RIVKA: Is he here? Is he the boss of you?

JOHANNA: He pays us—so yes.

RIVKA: Look at all us poor folk, eating out of the hands of the rich. The man's never set foot in your house and it's clear that he's still the master of it. You change your mind about the alcove, you let me know.

> RIVKA *heads back down the trap door.*

JOHANNA: Who says we have to give you something in exchange?

> RIVKA *stops.*

JOHANNA: Aren't we already giving you enough?

RIVKA: What, a three-foot crawl space? That would be an awfully expensive rent.

JOHANNA: Think you're worth that much, do you?

RIVKA: I'm not usually in the business of placing a value on it.

JOHANNA: Funny, isn't it. Just when the price of everything goes up, the price of a woman goes down.

Pause.

RIVKA: No. I won't. I want something for it.

JOHANNA: You have everything!

RIVKA: Like what?

JOHANNA: Food, every day. Food that my husband scrounges for.

RIVKA: Food. Now and then. Off a clean floor that we've slaved over.

JOHANNA: This is the thanks we get, is it? We could have turned you in for a profit.

RIVKA: You don't turn us in because you know they'll shoot you.

Silence.

JOHANNA: It must be nice, staying safe down there in your little nest—

RIVKA: You're one to talk. When's the last time you left this house, Johanna? What are you afraid of? You could run tomorrow as hard and as fast as you can in any direction. But you don't. And I'll never understand it. See, I hide because I have no choice. You hide because you're a coward.

Silence.

RIVKA: Again . . . you change your mind about the alcove? You let me know.

JOHANNA *goes to the curtains. Closes them.*

JOHANNA: Stand up.

RIVKA: I finally have your permission to stand, do I?

JOHANNA: Stand up.

RIVKA: What's the plan here? What are you going to do? You going to force me?

MAX: Rivka, I don't—

JOHANNA: Max.

RIVKA: Well?

Silence.

JOHANNA *faces her but does not move.*

RIVKA: What, am I going to have to walk you through how this works? If you mean business, go and get your husband's gun.

Silence.

RIVKA: I know you have a gun. I've seen it. And I know it's in the bin by the door. So go and get it, Johanna. If you're not going to bargain, at least give me a little incentive.

JOHANNA: No one is raising a gun in this house.

JOHANNA goes to RIVKA, gives her something tiny, wrapped in a piece of cloth. RIVKA opens it. Inside is . . .

RIVKA: Your sugar cube.

She lifts the sugar cube in her fingers like a diamond.

JOHANNA: Will you do it?

RIVKA looks from the sugar cube to JOHANNA. To MAX. She nods.

MAX: Johanna . . .

JOHANNA touches him like a mother touches a son.

JOHANNA: Let me take care of you.

MAX goes to RIVKA and offers her his hand. He helps her as she struggles to her feet. They move towards the bed. The trap door opens and ISAAC surfaces.

ISAAC: Rivka? Why are you . . .

ISAAC notices that MAX is holding RIVKA upright.

ISAAC: What are you doing?

RIVKA: I'm earning your breakfast.

JOHANNA: There is no breakfast.

MAX: Yes there is. We can't be wasteful.

JOHANNA *looks at the dog. Sighs. Turns to look for something.*

ISAAC: *(to* RIVKA*)* You can't do this.

RIVKA: Don't.

ISAAC: Rivka!

RIVKA: Do you have a better solution?

ISAAC *turns to* JOHANNA.

ISAAC: Johanna, do something.

JOHANNA *ignores him.*

ISAAC: Max . . .

MAX: Look, I'm not . . . I didn't . . .

ISAAC: You disgust me.

MAX *freezes.*

MAX: What did you say?

ISAAC: You heard me.

MAX: Have you forgotten whose house you're in?

ISAAC: Not for a moment.

MAX: You know, I've been very patient with you. I have been very patient.

ISAAC: Excuse me?

MAX: Here we are, all of us struggling tooth and nail to get by, and there you are, withholding from the group.

ISAAC: What are you talking about?

MAX: And here I am, trying to be the bigger person. I didn't want to ask because it's not the kind of thing you ask for. It's the kind of thing that any decent man offers.

ISAAC: I really don't know what you're talking about.

MAX: Your glasses.

Silence.

ISAAC: What about them?

MAX: There's a market for glasses.

ISAAC: I'm half-blind without them.

MAX: You'll starve with them.

ISAAC: I won't be able to read.

MAX: Know what you can't put in the belly?

ISAAC: What?

MAX: Books.

ISAAC: Please . . .

MAX: Give them to me.

ISAAC: No.

MAX: Give them to me!

> MAX *pounces on* ISAAC. ISAAC *struggles.* MAX *wins. He takes the eyeglasses. A moment of almost shared shame between them at the scuffle.*

ISAAC: Can we consider the debt paid?

MAX: Yes. For now.

ISAAC: Rivka, come.

RIVKA *doesn't move.*

ISAAC: You heard him. I've earned our keep. Come.

RIVKA: It wasn't just that.

ISAAC: What?

RIVKA: I made a deal.

ISAAC: What kind of deal?

RIVKA: A sugar cube.

ISAAC: Oh.

Pause.

ISAAC: Can I have it?

RIVKA *goes to him, crouches, brings her face close to his so he can see.*

RIVKA: He was right.

ISAAC: What?

RIVKA: You should have given up your glasses long ago.

RIVKA *places the sugar cube in her mouth. Stands and moves towards the bed.* JOHANNA *returns to the table with an axe. She looks at* ISAAC.

JOHANNA: I suggest you go back to sleep.

For a moment everyone is still. ISAAC *disappears again,
shutting the trap door.* MAX *sets the eyeglasses on the
table and goes to the bed.* JOHANNA *turns up the music.*
MAX *undoes his pants.* RIVKA *unbuttons her dress.*
JOHANNA *lifts the axe over the dog.*

Blackout.

SCENE 2

The next morning.

The sound of bombs in the distance. JOHANNA *is listening to the radio, setting the table.*

JOHANNA *reaches over, changes the channel. Classical music plays. She hums along and lays a plate of meat on the table.*

MAX: *(offstage)* Johanna . . .

MAX *enters. He stands in the doorway.*

JOHANNA: Good morning.

JOHANNA *kisses him.*

JOHANNA: Sit.

MAX *sits.* JOHANNA *slides a plate in front of him.*

JOHANNA: It's a dog's breakfast!

JOHANNA *smiles wildly, claps a hand over her mouth, stifles a laugh.*

MAX: Are you all right?

JOHANNA: I'm starving.

JOHANNA *sits. Picks up a fork.*

JOHANNA: He was such a good boy. Remember the—remember that time I fell through the ice? But your back was turned. But little Bernard barked with everything he had, didn't he? And he didn't stop—no, not until you reached down and pulled me up. Hardly took any time for the sleeve of my coat to freeze to the sleeve of your coat. Poor Bernard.

JOHANNA *stares at the meat on her fork.*

MAX: There's something that we need to discuss.

JOHANNA: There isn't. These are very strange times. I know that. If I didn't forgive everyone in sight, I'd probably go insane.

MAX: Not about that.

JOHANNA: What?

MAX: Someone sent word. On behalf of Helen's father.

JOHANNA: Yes, I wanted to talk to you about that. Yesterday I found a very condescending letter—

MAX: Helen's father was taken.

Silence.

JOHANNA: Dead?

MAX *shrugs.*

JOHANNA: What about the payments?

MAX *shakes his head.*

JOHANNA: Aren't you hungry?

MAX: I'm starving.

JOHANNA: Me too.

They sit. They don't eat.

MAX: Is there salt?

JOHANNA: No.

MAX: Oh, yes.

JOHANNA: Why? What's wrong with it?

MAX: Nothing. Haven't tasted it yet.

Silence.

JOHANNA: No reason why we can't all eat together, don't you think? Oh, but there are five of us. We only have four dishes. Well! Surely we have the decency to share.

JOHANNA *rises. Pulls open the trap door.*

JOHANNA: Rise and shine down there!

JOHANNA *goes to the cupboard, pushes it open.*

JOHANNA: Time to greet the day!

RIVKA *and* ISAAC *emerge.* HELEN *emerges.*

JOHANNA: I thought that it would be nice for us to all eat together again.

ISAAC: At the table?

JOHANNA: What are you, suicidal? Together as in, at the same time. Like a family. It'll be just like New Year's, like the time we all drank together. It's what Bernard would have wanted.

JOHANNA *sets a plate in front of* RIVKA, *a plate in front of* ISAAC. HELEN *crouches beside them.*

ISAAC: I can't sit up.

RIVKA: Lie on your stomach.

JOHANNA: I'm afraid that we haven't got enough dishes, Helen. You'll have to wait until someone is finished.

RIVKA: Is this your dog?

JOHANNA: Yes.

> RIVKA *and* ISAAC *look at one another. They begin to eat ravenously.* HELEN *watches.*

HELEN: Rivka, may I have a bite from your plate?

RIVKA: No.

HELEN: Isaac, may I have just a little bite from your plate?

RIVKA: Don't give her one, Isaac.

ISAAC: Sorry.

HELEN: Please, Johanna.

JOHANNA: Pardon me?

HELEN: Mrs. Darrow. I'm starving. My eyes are clouding over.

ISAAC: At least yours work.

JOHANNA: I told you, Helen, there aren't enough plates. You have to wait.

HELEN: I'll eat with my hands.

JOHANNA: That doesn't seem very refined.

HELEN: Please.

JOHANNA: Catch.

> JOHANNA *tosses a piece of meat high over* HELEN'*s head. It lands on the other side of the room.*

JOHANNA: Sorry. Not a good throw.

> HELEN *nearly trips over herself crawling to the meat. She picks it up off the ground, stuffs it in her mouth.*

JOHANNA: Good girl.

MAX: Helen, your father's dead.

HELEN: Who?

MAX: Your father.

HELEN: Oh, I see.

> *Pause.*

HELEN: Can I have another piece?

JOHANNA: That depends. Rivka earned their breakfasts. Yours hasn't been paid for.

HELEN: I haven't got any money.

JOHANNA: Give me your doll.

> HELEN *goes to retrieve her doll. She crawls to the table. Lays it beside* JOHANNA'*s untouched plate;* JOHANNA *hasn't eaten.* JOHANNA *puts a piece of meat in* HELEN'*s mouth.*

ISAAC: We should get the alcove.

MAX: What?

ISAAC: We earned it. The glasses and the other.

MAX: You earned your breakfast.

ISAAC: Helen hasn't earned anything. That doll is worthless.

HELEN: She isn't!

RIVKA: And Papa won't pay you now.

HELEN: Don't you talk about my papa!

> ISAAC *stops eating. Throughout the next section they all do, curling into themselves, sick.*

ISAAC: I'm going to be sick.

MAX: I think we'll all be sick.

RIVKA: Oh no.

HELEN: My belly hurts.

MAX: You know what you can't . . . you know what you can't put—

ISAAC: That's not right.

MAX: —in the belly?

RIVKA: Dog?

JOHANNA: Bernard was such a good dog, though.

MAX: . . . I forget now.

HELEN: Ow.

ISAAC: I ate too much.

They are all lying about the room, except JOHANNA. *She looks at the doll and picks it up, treating it like a doll. Then with the air of someone who is trying something out, she places the doll in her arms. She begins to gently rock it like a baby. She hums a lullaby.*

Blackout.

SCENE 3

The next morning.

MAX *sleeps at the table.* HELEN *sucks her thumb on the floor. The trap door is open and* RIVKA *peers intently into the hole.* JOHANNA *is on the bed, cradling the doll, now bundled in cloth.* ISAAC *is crawling about, searching for something. He arrives at* RIVKA *and pats her, identifying her.*

ISAAC: Have you got a pen?

RIVKA: No. Do you hear that?

ISAAC: What is it?

RIVKA: Music, I think.

ISAAC: No.

RIVKA: Coming from the sky . . .

RIVKA *puts her head down, listening.* ISAAC *moves, feeling about, finds* JOHANNA.

ISAAC: Have you got a pen?

JOHANNA: Helen has a pen.

JOHANNA *covers the baby's ears.*

JOHANNA: She wrote a very nasty letter with it.

ISAAC: Helen, where's your pen?

HELEN: In my house.

ISAAC *gropes his way towards the alcove.*

RIVKA: No one hears that?

MAX *sniffs the plate in front of him.*

MAX: Spoiled.

ISAAC: Is there paper?

JOHANNA: Helen has paper. She wrote a letter.

HELEN: There isn't any paper.

ISAAC: What happened to it?

HELEN: I . . . I ate it.

MAX: You should have shared.

HELEN: It wasn't very good.

MAX: Still.

HELEN: Why do you need it?

ISAAC: I ran out of books.

MAX: Did Helen eat them?

HELEN: No!

ISAAC: I thought I'd write one.

JOHANNA: Will you write a book for the baby?

ISAAC: For the baby . . .

JOHANNA: Yes, for the baby.

MAX: (*humouring*) He'd love to write a story for the baby. Wouldn't he?

ISAAC: There's no paper . . .

RIVKA: Use me.

> RIVKA *rolls up her sleeve and offers her forearm to him.*

ISAAC: Really?

RIVKA: I don't mind.

MAX: There you go!

> ISAAC *begins to write.*

RIVKA: Isaac knows every book. You should see him. He always said he'd write his own.

> *They begin to crowd towards* ISAAC.

HELEN: What's your story about?

ISAAC: Love.

RIVKA: They're all about love, aren't they?

HELEN: Will it be published?

RIVKA: You'll see it in every store window.

HELEN: Will you be famous?

ISAAC: Well . . .

JOHANNA: Famous. Imagine that.

MAX: And I'll say, I knew him! And no one will believe it.

HELEN: How does it start?

ISAAC: How do you think it should start?

HELEN: With food.

MAX: Definitely start with food!

ISAAC: (*squinting*) I can't see what I'm doing. This might not make sense.

RIVKA: Everyone will think you're smarter that way.

HELEN: What kind of food will it be?

ISAAC: The baby's favourite kind.

JOHANNA: What do you think, baby?

> *They all look at the doll, wait for the doll's answer.*

JOHANNA: Plums, is it? Oh, that's nice.

HELEN: I once had a plum cake on my birthday, I think.

JOHANNA: With three tiers. The baby remembers.

HELEN: Can it be about a birthday?

ISAAC: I've run out of room.

HELEN: Use me!

> HELEN *offers her forearm.* ISAAC *begins to write.*

ISAAC: Once upon a time, on a little girl's birthday—

HELEN: Can her name be Helen?

ISAAC: Once upon a time, on Helen's birthday—

HELEN: (*to the others, glowing*) I'm a character.

ISAAC: —She had a grand party. And there was a buffet table, filled with food. It was the most extravagant thing she'd ever seen.

JOHANNA: Oh my goodness.

MAX: Imagine.

JOHANNA: What was on the table?

ISAAC: Fresh bread.

JOHANNA: Bread!

RIVKA: What else?

ISAAC: Caviar.

HELEN: Caviar . . .

MAX: May I have some of the story?

> MAX *rolls up his sleeve, offers his arm to* ISAAC, *who begins to write on him.*

MAX: What else, do you think? Wheels of cheese?

ISAAC: Definitely wheels of cheese.

MAX: I thought so.

ISAAC: But that's not all.

HELEN: What do you mean? There's more food, right?

ISAAC: That's just it. It's all food.

HELEN: What?

ISAAC: Everything is food.

RIVKA: I don't understand.

ISAAC: That's the story. Everything is food!

RIVKA: Oh, that's good. That's really good.

HELEN: I love this story!

JOHANNA: May I have some, Max, if you're finished?

MAX: Help yourself.

JOHANNA *offers her forearm.* ISAAC *writes.*

HELEN: So the table that the food is on—

ISAAC: Is also food.

JOHANNA: What flavour?

ISAAC: The best flavour.

HELEN: And the floor?

ISAAC: The floor is even better than the table.

RIVKA: You know what? It probably tastes like icing.

HELEN: Probably.

ISAAC: So the people ate and ate, and even though the food on the table disappeared, they just kept eating. They ate the table. They ate the floors. They ate the walls and the roof and the light fixtures.

HELEN: And then what happened? When they ran out?

ISAAC *starts to write on his own forearm.*

ISAAC: Then . . . then they began to eat each other.

HELEN: The people were food!?

ISAAC: Were they ever!

RIVKA: Yes! Oooh, that's really good.

MAX: Oh, excellent.

JOHANNA: I love this story.

HELEN: What did they taste like? The people?

ISAAC: They tasted like meat!

RIVKA: What part did they eat first?

ISAAC: Everyone started with a finger. For practical reasons, you know?

MAX: Yes, I could live without a finger. Smart people.

JOHANNA: But you use your hands, Max. You care for the chickens. How would you hold the pail of feed?

RIVKA: She has a point.

JOHANNA: I could stand to lose a finger.

ISAAC: But Johanna, you cook. You need to hold a knife.

MAX: And she has the baby to care for now, doesn't she?

RIVKA: Yes she does.

ISAAC: I'd eat my finger. I don't think I'd mind.

JOHANNA: But how would you write?

RIVKA: She's right. You'd never finish the story without a finger. But me . . .

ISAAC: But what about your violin? How would you play?

RIVKA: I haven't played the violin in so long.

JOHANNA: Oh, but you will again.

MAX: Yes, you need your fingers for music.

HELEN: You know what? I don't need any of my fingers, really. I've never used them a day in my life.

JOHANNA: They're very pretty fingers, Helen.

HELEN: Do you think?

JOHANNA: Oh yes. They're extraordinary.

MAX: Really, really something.

HELEN: Thank you!

JOHANNA: Still young.

RIVKA: Fresh.

HELEN: You know what? Why don't I share? It is my party, after all.

JOHANNA: Oh no, Helen, we couldn't.

HELEN: I have five fingers, and there are five of us. It's what a polite host would do.

JOHANNA: It is, isn't it?

HELEN: Of course!

JOHANNA: That's hospitality, see.

HELEN: Which one is nicer—left or right? They're both nice, aren't they?

RIVKA: It's hard to say. They're both really beautiful hands.

HELEN: Oh, thank you. Thank you so much!

RIVKA: They're exquisite.

HELEN: When I look at them this way, I think I prefer the right, but when I look at them this way (*flips hands*), I think the left one is a little better, don't you think?

MAX: Yes, left, I think.

RIVKA: Left.

JOHANNA: I agree.

ISAAC: Who gets first pick?

MAX: Well, they're Helen's fingers.

RIVKA: But whoever does the cutting gets first pick.

ISAAC: Why?

RIVKA: Because that's the rule.

HELEN: She's right. That's the rule.

JOHANNA: Should we do it at the table?

MAX: No, she's not allowed to sit at the table.

JOHANNA: The curtains are closed.

MAX: They look open to me.

JOHANNA: Come here, Helen! Here, good girl!

> HELEN *crawls to the table.* JOHANNA *takes her left hand and places it flat on the table.*

RIVKA: What should we use?

MAX: There's an axe.

RIVKA: Who cuts?

ISAAC: I'd like to, if no one objects. It is my story.

MAX: That sounds fair.

> ISAAC *gropes blindly for the axe. He picks up the doll instead and wields it like an axe.*

JOHANNA: No, that's the baby!

> MAX *passes* ISAAC *the axe.*

MAX: Here.

ISAAC: Where's her hand?

> RIVKA *reaches for* ISAAC'*s hand. Rests it on* HELEN'*s.*

ISAAC: Oh, I can almost see it.

> *Everyone stands back.* ISAAC *raises the axe over his head. Suddenly there is the sound of faint music.*

RIVKA: There it is again!

ISAAC: I hear it.

RIVKA: I knew you would eventually.

MAX: Clear as a bell.

HELEN: I hear it too.

JOHANNA: And me.

> *Pause.*

JOHANNA: It's beautiful.

HELEN: It's like a party.

JOHANNA: Like winter on the lake.

HELEN: It's perfect music for my party . . . Look!

> HELEN *points into the open trap door. They all walk towards it, gazing inside. A blue silk dress floats out of the hole.* HELEN *catches it. She sighs with delight and holds it to her chest. A lighting transition—something to indicate a change of reality. The axe disappears.* HELEN *and* JOHANNA, *alone.*

HELEN: I love it. It's the colour of . . . oh, what are those tiny flowers? Those ones we saw last spring, that day we went for a drive in Father's new car . . . not bluebells . . . the ones with the little yellow eyes. Forget-me-nots! Forget-me-not blue. Does it flatter me?

JOHANNA: Yes, darling Helen.

HELEN: Does it make my eyes look blue?

JOHANNA: In this light.

HELEN: It's so much nicer than the one Father picked out. He should know that I'm not a child anymore.

JOHANNA: He knows. He just doesn't like it.

HELEN: Puffed sleeves make my arms look fat.

JOHANNA: You aren't fat, child.

HELEN: I should eat less.

HELEN *twirls with the dress.*

HELEN: It's a good length for dancing.

JOHANNA: Don't dance too much.

HELEN: *(whining)* Mother! I'm not a baby!

MAX *appears.*

HELEN: Father, look. Look at me. Look! Admit it. This one's better.

MAX: I suppose it's very pretty.

JOHANNA: Helen looks just like a woman.

MAX: There's a boy here to see you. But nothing funny, understand?

HELEN: Stop it, I'm a grown-up.

ISAAC *appears.*

ISAAC: Hello, Helen. I brought you a corsage.

ISAAC *holds up a length of rope.*

JOHANNA: It's very lovely.

MAX: A gentleman with a gentleman's taste.

HELEN: I love it. You should put it on.

HELEN *holds up her wrist.* ISAAC *ties it around her upper arm.*

HELEN: Wait. They go on the wrist, don't they? Mother?

JOHANNA: Not today, Helen.

ISAAC *pulls the rope tight.*

HELEN: It's very tight. I'm not sure if I can dance this way.

MAX: It needs to be tighter, I think.

RIVKA *appears. She is eating a slab of cake.*

RIVKA: *(to* HELEN*)* He likes you, I think. He was watching you all night.

HELEN: Really? Do you think?

RIVKA: This cake is so good.

HELEN: You shouldn't have that. I didn't cut it yet.

RIVKA: The boy will cut it for you.

HELEN: But it's my birthday.

JOHANNA: But then you won't get to be the one who chooses, Helen. Those are the rules.

MAX *appears with the axe.*

HELEN: Maybe . . . maybe we should dance first.

ISAAC: Why?

HELEN *and* ISAAC *dance.*

MAX: Not so close.

MAX, JOHANNA, *and* RIVKA *watch as they dance.* RIVKA *eats cake.* MAX *and* JOHANNA *clap.*

ISAAC: Come now.

ISAAC *takes* HELEN *by the hand.*

HELEN: Where are we going?

ISAAC: You made a promise.

HELEN: No I didn't.

ISAAC: You said you'd be mine.

HELEN: Really? What did Father say?

ISAAC: He told me to cut the cake.

> ISAAC *kisses* HELEN *and lowers her to the floor. He takes her hand and straightens one arm to her side.*

HELEN: Be careful with it. It's a three-tiered plum cake with—

HELEN & RIVKA: —buttercream icing.

> MAX *passes* ISAAC *the axe.*

ISAAC: Don't worry. I'll probably miss.

> RIVKA *sets a cake on the table.*

JOHANNA: It looks so fresh.

ISAAC: Does it matter where?

RIVKA: Just so long as there's frosting for everyone.

ISAAC: Happy birthday, Helen.

> ISAAC *raises the axe.*
>
> *Blackout.*
>
> *Explosions.*

SCENE 4

An indiscernible amount of time has passed.

Darkness. Continuous, deafening explosions. Lights rise.
A disaster zone. Dust in the air. Furniture overturned.
JOHANNA *sits under the table, rocking the doll.* MAX *lies*
on the bed. ISAAC *is face down beside his plate.* HELEN *is*
in RIVKA'*s lap.* RIVKA *strokes her hair.* HELEN *sucks her*
thumb, the other arm in a crude sling. After a little while
the bombs fade. Complete silence. ISAAC *rouses.*

ISAAC: When is it?

RIVKA: Don't know.

ISAAC: How long?

RIVKA: Don't know.

ISAAC *moves. Knocks his dish.*

ISAAC: What's that?

RIVKA: Dish of dog.

ISAAC *sniffs his plate.*

ISAAC: Rotting.

HELEN *feels her clothing.*

HELEN: Why am I wet?

RIVKA: Your hand.

HELEN: Not that kind of wet. It's all wet.

MAX rises.

MAX: What's that sound?

ISAAC: Nothing.

HELEN: I'm hungry.

HELEN reaches for a piece of meat on the floor. RIVKA slaps her hand.

RIVKA: Don't eat that.

HELEN: Ow.

HELEN starts to cry.

JOHANNA: Can the baby eat it?

HELEN: I want her back.

JOHANNA: You traded.

MAX: What's that sound?

All listen. Silence.

RIVKA: Nothing.

JOHANNA: Nothing at all.

ISAAC: Quiet.

RIVKA: Is it over?

MAX: Maybe . . .

RIVKA: Check!

MAX *takes the radio. Switches it on. Static. He sits down to fiddle with it.*

JOHANNA: When is it?

ISAAC: Don't know.

JOHANNA: Morning?

RIVKA: Don't know.

JOHANNA: Evening?

RIVKA: Shut up.

> JOHANNA *looks at her wrist. She laughs.*

HELEN: What's funny?

JOHANNA: I've never owned a watch.

MAX: Broken.

> MAX *sets down the radio. Goes to the window.*

JOHANNA: What's there?

RIVKA: Anyone?

MAX: Fire.

ISAAC: Big?

MAX: Just embers now.

> *The sound of church bells. All listen.*

ISAAC: What's that?

RIVKA: You hear it too?

ISAAC: Thought it was my ears ringing.

MAX: Does it mean . . .

The bells toll. It sinks in.

RIVKA: Do you hear those bells, Helen?

HELEN: Is it heaven?

RIVKA: No. That means it's over!

HELEN: Over?

Pause.

HELEN: What does that mean?

RIVKA: It means . . . it means that someday soon you'll have a duck with spring greens again.

HELEN: That's good. I'm so hungry.

MAX rises, goes to the table. Crouches to speak to JOHANNA.

MAX: Do you hear that, Johanna? It's safe now! We're all safe! You can come out!

MAX helps JOHANNA out. He kisses her. He holds out a hand to ISAAC, still on the floor.

ISAAC: I can't.

MAX: Come on, boy, you're safe now! Adrenaline will see you through!

MAX helps ISAAC to his feet. ISAAC stands wobbly but firm. MAX shakes his hand. JOHANNA and MAX go to HELEN and RIVKA and help them to their feet. They all begin to hug and kiss.

MAX: Who would have thought, eh? Who would have thought we'd have seen it through to the bitter end? But here we all are, all of us together. Alive. Except for Bernard. But all of us, we're alive. We're safe.

JOHANNA: It's a celebration! There ought to have been a bottle of champagne.

MAX: We can pretend, eh? Like we did at New Year's.

JOHANNA: There's no glass. And no water.

MAX: Look! Look at that, Johanna! One of them survived!

MAX points. In the rubble is a lone wine glass, standing upright, filled with water.

MAX: Now that's a sign if there ever was one.

RIVKA: How is there water?

JOHANNA: It's a miracle for the new year.

MAX retrieves the glass.

MAX: It's like you always used to say, didn't you, Johanna?

JOHANNA: What did I say?

MAX: Good people will receive good rewards.

JOHANNA: I'd forgotten that I used to say that.

MAX: This, this is the real start of the New Year, isn't it? This is the real beginning. It's the end of an era.

ISAAC: We'll begin again.

RIVKA: A fresh start.

MAX: To the new year.

He raises his glass.

MAX: Cheers.

MAX drinks. Passes the glass to JOHANNA. She drinks. Passes the glass, which continues to be passed among them. JOHANNA begins to hum the tune of "Auld Lang Syne" as the glass is passed—the humming is faint at first, but then stronger. The others, except HELEN, begin to join in with words.

ALL: *Should old acquaintance be forgot*
And never brought to mind
Should old acquaintance be forgot
And auld lang syne

For auld lang syne, my dear
For auld lang syne,
We'll take a cup of kindness yet
For auld lang syne . . .

As they are singing, HELEN goes to the potato bin, retrieves the revolver. They see this and stop singing. Without a word, she turns the gun on JOHANNA and MAX.

JOHANNA: Helen . . .

ISAAC: What are you doing?

HELEN: I want my doll back.

All are frozen. RIVKA steps forward.

RIVKA: Well, that isn't how you go about getting it. We aren't barbarians.

MAX: Certainly not.

RIVKA takes the gun from HELEN's hand and lays it on the table.

HELEN: How do I get it back, then?

ISAAC: You ask.

RIVKA: Politely.

HELEN: *(to JOHANNA)* Give—
(to RIVKA) How do I do that?

RIVKA whispers in her ear.

RIVKA: Go on.

HELEN: *(like she's trying out new words)* Johanna, may I have my doll back, please?

JOHANNA: Of course, dear. All you had to do was ask.

JOHANNA places the doll carefully in HELEN's arms.

HELEN: *(to RIVKA, a loud whisper)* How do I pay her?

RIVKA: Don't be silly.

JOHANNA: Of course you don't pay me. It's yours.

HELEN: Oh . . . I'm confused.

ISAAC: You'll get the hang of it.

Suddenly it begins to snow inside the house—the rooftop has been blown away.

RIVKA: Look at that!

ISAAC: What is it?

ISAAC looks up, squinting.

RIVKA: Sky.

ISAAC: (*feeling the snow*) Snow?

HELEN: Snow!

They watch it fall a moment.

RIVKA: We should be going.

HELEN: Me too?

ISAAC: Yes.

HELEN: Where will we go?

JOHANNA: Oh, won't you stay for dinner first?

MAX: Yes, stay! Shall we?

MAX pulls a chair from the table, gestures for HELEN, RIVKA, and ISAAC to sit.

MAX: Guests first. Come everyone, sit! Sit down! There you go!

They all sit.

JOHANNA: After you, Helen.

HELEN looks at the bare table, confused. Then she looks up. Understands. She opens her mouth, catches a snowflake.

JOHANNA: How is it?

HELEN: Delicious.

They all open their mouths to catch the falling snow.

Blackout.

END OF PLAY

ACKNOWLEDGEMENTS

Hunger was developed with the support and creative input of many people. A special thank you to Ruth Lawrence and Michael Waller, who were there from the beginning and integral to the script's development and production.

Thank you to Todd Hennessey, Adam Brake, Des Walsh, Leah Pritchard, Emma Anderson, and Rory Lambert, who all contributed to early script development.

Many thanks to the original cast, crew, and creative team for helping the play find its shape in rehearsal and onstage: Marthe Bernard, Ruth Lawrence, Greg Malone, Jamie Mac, Michael Waller, Lois Brown, Jamie Skidmore, Melanie Ozon, Mara Bredovskis, Karl Simmons, Erin Normandeau, Katie Butler Major, and Perfect Day.

Thank you to Remzi Cej for sharing his lived experience.

Thanks to Santiago Guzmán, Nina John, Deidre Gillard-Rowlings, Emily Austin, Sheldon Downey, Vaida V. Nairn, Victoria Wells, Susan Kelsey, and Renée Hackett, who came onboard for the provincial tour and gave it a second life.

In 2016, *Hunger* was a nominee for the RBC Tarragon Emerging Playwright Prize. Thank you to Amy House for placing my work in the running.

Eternal gratitude to White Rooster and Rising Tide Theatre for bringing *Hunger* to the stage, and to the Newfoundland and Labrador Arts and Culture Centres for helping to bring it on the road.

Thank you to Robert Chafe for the careful eye and thoughtful suggestions, Claire Wilkshire for the attention to detail, and to Breakwater for putting it into print. Thank you to Mallory Fisher for being my constant sounding board.

The premiere production of *Hunger* was supported by the Canada Council for the Arts, the City of St. John's, and ArtsNL.

MEGHAN GREELEY is a writer, performer, and director originally from Corner Brook, Newfoundland and Labrador. Her work has been published in *The Breakwater Book of Contemporary Newfoundland Plays* (vol. 1) and the Playwrights Canada Press anthology *Long Story Short*. She was a 2016 nominee for the RBC Tarragon Emerging Playwrights Prize and completed artist residencies at the Tarragon Playwrights Unit and Nightwood Theatre's Write from the Hip program. Her stage plays have been produced in Toronto, Halifax, and Calgary, and across the island of Newfoundland.